VOLUME 2

Begin in English

More
Vocabulary-Expanding
Short Stories
for
Launched Beginners

Stories by Judith Bailey

Illustrations by Meredith Kraike

Procedures by Joan Ashkenas, Editor

JAG PUBLICATIONS

Published by:
 JAG Publications
11288 Ventura Blvd.
Studio City, CA 91604
Telephone and Fax: (818) 505-9002

Design by Words & Deeds, Los Angeles

Printed in the United States of America

10   9   8   7   6   5   4   3

Library of Congress catalog card no. 87-81968

ISBN 0-943327-11-3

FOREWORD: To the Instructor

This second volume of *Begin in English* offers the same type of high-interest short stories at the same level as the first volume. Since subject matter is different here, different vocabulary is employed, and consequently, vocabulary expansion is further enhanced. As before, the object is to give students words to express themselves, by reading, writing and conversing.

These fourteen stories are designed for easy, entertaining reading by launched beginners of English: for those who now have some English vocabulary and are familiar with the present tense. The stories have all been tested in the classroom. One of the great delights for my students, and for me, was their discovery that they already knew enough English to read an entire story.

Subject matter is quite varied. There are folk tales and urban legends retold, human interest stories, some humor, some biography, history and even a mystery. A major attribute of all of them is that they really give the student something of substance to read—a short story or play, rather than simply a paragraph or two.

It hardly needs to be argued that these days our classrooms are filled with students from a multitude of language backgrounds. But teachers, generally, are not multi-lingual. It follows then, that we teachers can help our students help themselves by becoming adept at using the dictionary. Students are provided here with a useful beginner's vocabulary, and emphasis is placed on teaching and encouraging use of the bilingual dictionary.

Not necessarily second in order of importance is that familiarity with the dictionary is basic to literacy. Although most foreign language students use bilingual dictionaries at beginning levels of their studies, some do not know how. I feel very strongly that these students should own them, and be taught to use them right away. I say this first as a foreign language student, and only second as a language teacher. Admittedly, it can be intrusive to stop and slavishly consult the dictionary for each word. But frequently, context conveys meaning, making it unnecessary to look up every unfamiliar word. This is ideal, but not always the case, and students indeed need to look up new words from time to time. There is really nothing like it for rapidly increasing vocabulary and getting on with the story.

REGARDING DICTIONARY WORK

Because I feel it is so important that students be comfortable with the dictionary, I have included at the beginning of the book a step-by-step dictionary lesson. It assumes that the student needs help with the basic concept of alphabetizing. I found that this part is very easily understood, and paves the way for the next part, "Using the Dictionary." During the lesson I work closely with the students and read along with them, pointing out the words and letters of the words they are looking up, so they may grasp the idea of alphabetical order. It may take up to an hour or so to teach, depending on the student's background, and on class size. But the rewards of this exercise will be immediately evident.

REGARDING VOCABULARY AND WORD LISTS

The vocabulary contained here is highly controlled. It includes words from the *The 2,000 Most Frequently Used Words In English*, edited by Robert J. Dixson. In this resource, the first 500 words follow the Thorndike-Lorge list. The second 500 words were derived, with some modification, mainly from the *Interim Report On Vocabulary Selection For Teaching Of English As A Foreign Language* (Palmer, Thorndike, West, Sapir, etc.). The remaining 1000 words of this list were compiled from Thorndike, emphasizing assessed needs for teaching conversation in English to primary level students.

In order to facilitate the reading and augment the word list, there has also been included vocabulary from the *Oxford Picture Dictionary of American*

English. Obviously, a picture dictionary, whatever its limits, is "universal": using pictures labeled in English to serve ESL students of every language background. An Oxford Picture Dictionary is provided with each class set of books, to be used as a general resource text. Nearly all of the words used in the word list, and those which are most likely to be new to some students, are found in one or both of these resources.

The beautiful illustrations that accompany the stories are also designed to convey meaning.

In addition to this, for the benefit of Spanish speakers, there has been a special effort made to use cognates. Cognates are veritable vehicles for transferring similarities: psychological frames of reference, making for real ease of comprehension.

A comprehensive word list at the back of the book indicates which words are found in Dixson's high frequency list, which in Oxford's Picture Dictionary, and which are cognates of Spanish.

Stories are told in the present tense, and in the future using "going to", since these tenses are stressed during the first year of studies. The exercises here are not strictly "grammar work". That remains the burden of the core text being used in class. Instead, the focus is on vocabulary expansion, with dictionary work implied, reading comprehension and discussion.

My advanced beginning students have enjoyed these stories. More than that—they have clamored for them! I truly believe yours will, too.

Joan Ashkenas, Editor

PROCEDURE

READING

It is suggested that students be allowed to read the story through silently. Then, they may re-read it to pick out the unfamiliar vocabulary. Usually, upon this second reading, much will be understood through context and by reference to the illustrations. After that, students should be encouraged to look up words independently in the dictionary. For the first story or so, you may wish to offer extra help to those students with newly acquired dictionary skills. Then, you might ask the class to follow along as you read aloud. For extra practice, students can be asked to each read a passage orally, around the room. The large illustrations preceding each story work well at this point for group discussions. They mainly depict pivotal scenes. Students might be asked questions: "who?", "what?", "where?", "when?". Or they could be asked to describe scenes in their own words, saying, "This is a..." "I can see some..."

EXERCISES

I. Vocabulary List. The words selected here for study should be quite familiar after the readings and the dictionary work. They are listed to ensure that is the case. Also, some words are used again in successive stories in slightly different contexts.

II. Definitions. (See Answer Key at back of book). A real opportunity for vocabulary expansion is in this exercise. Here, the most challenging words from the above list have been selected. For students who wish to do so, a chance is provided to explore the dictionary and learn synonyms for words they have now studied.

You may wish students to check their own work, but you may find it preferable to discuss the answers with the class as a whole, since many of the words have multiple usage.

III. Reading Comprehension. (See Answer Key at back of book.) This exercise consists of questions to be answered by referring to the story and copying the correct passage. Its purpose is for practice in writing and spelling, as well as for comprehension. As in Exercise II above, you may want students to check their own work.

IV. Discussion. Students are asked to look at pictures and, using the vocabulary, answer questions. These are especially good for paired students, but can be used for group work as well. Students should have acquired some confidence after the initial readings and vocabulary drill, to talk with others about the situations and characters.

V. Writing. After the above oral work, students are asked to perform some original written exercises: (a) to list several things about the story or characters. In answering these, some students may be able and motivated to use original language. Others could answer the questions according to their ability, in just a word or short phrase from the story itself. You will have to be the judge of individual competency. But, since enjoyment of reading is of primary consideration here, you may not want to frighten off less able students with an exacting writing requirement. Or (b) to write from dictation. For this, ask students to study a particular paragraph from the story, then close the book and write as you dictate. This might be a new activity for many. It is suggested that each sentence be repeated slowly, first all the way through, and then in short phrases. It may be necessary to read it a third time. Advise students to note spelling and punctuation, especially if dialogue is included.

AS A COMPLEMENT TO THE LAUBACH METHOD:

Begin in English, though designed for non-English-speaking students, can also be used effectively by English speakers for remedial work in basic reading, writing and spelling. It is particularly appropriate for students of the Laubach Method at Skill Book levels 2 and 3. This book's added dimension is that it teaches and encourages use of the foreign student's own bilingual dictionary, or the native speaker's English dictionary.

A great number of the chart-listed skills at levels 2 and 3 are again introduced or reinforced here. The exercises test reading comprehension, and offer practice in spelling. Writing practice is provided, sometimes by dictation, sometimes by copying sentences for reinforcement, sometimes by referring to the text, other times in original sentences, as individual abilities allow.

The underlying intent here is, as in the Laubach Method, motivation of independent learning with a minimum of teaching help.

CONTENTS

Learning to Use the Dictionary

I ALPHABETIZING

Use the alphabet to help you do the following exercises.

a b c d e f g h i j k l m n o p q r s t u v w x y z

1. Put these letters in correct order:

    b c a_____ _____ _____
    i g h_____ _____ _____
    o m n_____ _____ _____

2. Put these words in correct order according to their first letters:

| sit | baby | light | house | _____ _____ _____ _____ |
| fast | apple | cake | down | _____ _____ _____ _____ |

3. These words have the same first letter. Arrange them according to their second letters:

buy	big	boy		_____ _____ _____
pin	pan	put	pet	_____ _____ _____ _____
shell	sell	spell		_____ _____ _____

4. These words begin with the same two letters. Put them in order according to their third letters:

plan	plum	plot	_____ _____ _____
flock	flake	flute	_____ _____ _____
street	stamp	stop	_____ _____ _____
through	thought	thin	_____ _____ _____

II USING THE DICTIONARY

Open the dictionary to where the letter 'b' begins. Notice that the first words you see following the 'b' all have 'a' for their second letter. Now look at their third letter. Notice that these third letters follow in alphabetical order: first 'a', then 'b', then 'c', through the rest of the alphabet. Using this idea, let's practice and look up the following words: baby, back, bad, bag.

Now turn the pages and pass the letters 'ba' until you find words beginning with 'be.' Look up these words: beach, bed, before, begin.

Now continue turning pages until you find words starting with 'bi.' Find these words: bicycle, big, bill, bird.

Now look for these words: black, boat, brake, bud.

III DICTIONARY WORK

Open the dictionary and look at the top of any page. You can see two words in dark letters. The word on the left gives you the first word on the page. The word on the right gives you the last word on the page, and between these, all words are in alphabetical order, according to their second, third, fourth, etc. letters.

Let's practice finding some words. Turn to the letter 'b' and look for the word 'bad.' You know it is close to the beginning of the 'b' because its second letter is 'a.' It comes after words beginning with 'bab' and 'bac' because 'b' and 'c' come before 'd' in the alphabet.

Let's try another word. Turn to the letter 'n' and find the word 'not.' The second letter, 'o', of 'not' is more towards the middle of the alphabet, so you must pass words beginning with 'na', 'ne', 'ni', and find words beginning with 'no.' Now you need to find the third letter, 't', after the 'o.' Look for it in its alphabetical order at the top of the pages in dark letters.

Using what you know, you can now look up any new words in the dictionary as you read.

"When I learn English, I'm going to teach it to you."

The Little Teacher

On the day she is fifty years old, Chen Lin-mei gets a present from her son. He sends her an airplane ticket to come to America. The son, Chen Yu-jen, is studying to be a doctor at a hospital in Boston. He wants his mother to live with him.

Lin-mei is sad to leave her village in China. But she is a widow. Yu-jen is her only child. She says good-bye to her friends and flies to Boston.

Yu-jen's tiny apartment seems wonderful to Lin-mei. Water comes out of a pipe, right into the kitchen. There is also a big, white machine to keep food cold. But Lin-mei is not really happy. She doesn't speak English. She doesn't know anybody. Yu-jen is hardly ever home. Most nights, he has to sleep at the hospital.

"Mother," Yu-jen tells her, "you must go to school and learn English. That is the way to make new friends."

"My son, I am too old to learn English," Lin-mei says.

Her days are long and lonely. She has nothing to do in Boston. Every day, Lin-mei takes a walk. She doesn't walk far because she is afraid of getting lost. One day, a little boy walks along with her. Lin-mei remembers him. He is the child with brown skin and black hair who lives in the apartment below. The boy wears his door key on a string around his neck. His mother seems to be away from home most of the time.

As they walk, the boy holds Lin-mei's hand. "I can't speak English yet," he tells her in Spanish. "Can you speak Spanish?" She doesn't understand a word he says. "Can you speak English?" he asks in Spanish. She doesn't understand that either. He shakes his head wisely. "I see that you can't," he says. "Don't worry. My mother is taking me to school tomorrow. When I learn English, I'm going to teach it to you."

A few days later, the boy rings Lin-mei's doorbell. He gives her a really big smile. He points to himself. "Javier," he says slowly and carefully. He adds, in

English, "My—name—is—Javier." The woman understands that he is teaching her his name. She points to herself. "Lin-mei," she says, but she can't remember the rest of it.

Javier is a hard-working teacher. He points to the window, the table, a chair, and teaches Lin-mei their English names. She repeats after him, "Window, table, chair." He tries to trick her. He points to the chair and says table. But Lin-mei is not easy to fool. She laughs and knocks on the table. "Table," she says.

Every day, after school, Javier teaches Lin-mei the new English words he is learning. He is a good teacher and she is a good student. They are becoming good friends. Sometimes Lin-mei gives the little boy Chinese cookies. They taste funny at first, but after a while he likes them.

One afternoon, Javier comes to Lin-mei's apartment with tears on his face and blood on his knee. She washes the cut carefully. Then she holds him and sings a soft Chinese song to him. Soon Javier feels better.

The next evening, Javier's mother comes to Lin-mei's door. Vera is a pretty young woman who works in a shirt factory. She brings with her a Chinese woman who works there too. The Chinese friend is able to tell Lin-mei how much Vera thanks her for her kindness to Javier. She tells Lin-mei that Javier and his mother are from Mexico. Javier's father is dead. She also asks Lin-mei if she can take care of Javier on evenings when Vera wants to go to school. Vera is learning English. At the same time, she wants to study to become a worker in a laboratory. She can't let Javier be alone at night. Lin-mei gladly agrees to take care of Javier.

That night, to Lin-mei's surprise, Yu-jen is able to come home to eat dinner and to sleep in his own bed.

"Maybe I am not too old to learn English," Lin-mei tells her son.

Soon, when Javier goes to his school, proudly carrying his books, Lin-mei goes to her school, proudly carrying her books. In school she meets all kinds of people from far away countries. They are learning English, just as she is.

Suddenly Lin-mei discovers that there are many interesting things to do in Boston. She also find a Chinese market, only a few blocks away from her house.

"Why don't I cook a Chinese dinner?" Lin-mei thinks. "I can invite the Russian lady from my class who lives around the corner. I can invite Javier and Vera and Yu-jen."

When Lin-mei invites Javier, his dark eyes shine like stars. "I love you, Lin-mei," he says in English. Lin-mei isn't sure what the word "love" means. Then Javier hugs her tight with his thin little arms, and she knows.

Exercises

I. Vocabulary

You probably know many of these words from reading the story and looking at the pictures. If there are still some you don't know, look them up in your dictionary now.

present	hospital	wisely	tears
ticket	key	repeat	blood
sad	proud	trick	discover
widow	shake	knock	invite

II. Definitions

Try to guess the best definition for these words. Then look them up in your dictionary and draw a circle around the answer.

1. a present
   a. a game
   b. a gift
   c. a gate

2. wisely
   a. unknowingly
   b. foolishly
   c. knowingly

3. repeat
   a. copy
   b. agree
   c. remove

4. proud(ly)
   a. being pleased with oneself
   b. being surprised
   c. being lonely

5. to trick
   a. to forgive
   b. to follow
   c. to fool

6. knock
   a. bend
   b. beat
   c. bite

III. Reading Comprehension

Read the questions. Find the answers in the story. Write the answers under the questions.

1. What present does Chen Lin-mei get from her son?

   _____

   _____

2. How does Lin-mei know the little boy who walks with her?

   _____

   _____

3. What does Javier do every day after school?

   _____

   _____

4. How does Lin-mei help Vera and Javier?

   _____

   _____

5. What does Lin-mei discover when she gets to English class?

   _____

   _____

6. What does Lin-mei think of doing for her new friends?

   _____

   _____

IV. Discussion
Look at the pictures. Talk to your partner. Use words from the story.

Picture #1.
What is Javier doing with Lin-Mei?
What does he say? What does she say?

Picture #2.
Who are the two women at Lin-mei's door?
What are they talking about?

V. Writing

What two things seem wonderful to Lin-mei about her son's apartment?

1. _____

2. _____

Write three things you know about Javier's mother, Vera.

1. _____

2. _____

3. _____

He sees a little black face with bright green eyes looking at him.

20

Lucky and Unlucky

His name is Luis Lopez, but his friends call him "Lucky." They call him that because he is always finding things. Once he finds twenty dollars in the street. Another time he finds a camera in the park. One Sunday, he finds a diamond ring in the sand at the beach. Lucky puts an advertisement in the newspaper. The ad tells about the lost ring, but nobody calls to ask for it. Lucky doesn't know what to do with the ring. He doesn't know any woman he wants to give it to. He hides it in a safe place and after a while he forgets about it.

Lucky is an automobile mechanic. He works downtown, in a busy garage. Everybody at the garage calls him Lucky, too.

Sometimes Lucky thinks to himself, "I don't feel very lucky. I'm not rich. I'm losing my hair. I'm almost forty years old and I still don't have a wife or a family. What's so lucky about that?"

One day, Lucky eats lunch in a Chinese restaurant. The waiter brings tea and a fortune cookie. Lucky breaks open the cookie. He reads his fortune on the little piece of paper that is inside. "YOU ARE GOING TO HAVE VERY GOOD LUCK," the paper says. Lucky laughs and eats his cookie. He hopes the fortune is true.

After lunch, while he walks back to the garage, he looks around to see if good luck is waiting for him. Maybe he is going to find money again. He doesn't see anything except a small, black cat. The little cat is following Lucky.

"Go home, cat," says Lucky. But the cat follows him.

"Get away! Don't you know that black cats are supposed to bring bad luck?"

The black cat disappears. An hour later, when Lucky is lying under a car that he is fixing, he sees a little black face with bright green eyes looking at him. The cat is under the car with him. The other mechanics start to laugh, and Lucky can't help laughing, too.

"What's your cat's name?" one of the men asks.

"It's not my cat," he answers, "but I think a good name for it is "Unlucky'."

Unlucky lies down in a corner of the garage and goes to sleep.

"What am I going to do with you?" Lucky asks Unlucky when it is time to lock up the garage and go home. "I don't want a cat. I'm going to put an ad in the newspaper. Maybe somebody owns you and wants you back."

Lucky and Unlucky go home together. Unlucky likes Lucky's apartment. She eats a can of tuna fish for dinner and goes to sleep on Lucky's bed.

"No," says Lucky, "this bed is just for me." He puts the cat on the floor. When he wakes up in the morning, Unlucky is sleeping on the bed, right next to him.

Lucky pays for an advertisement in the newspaper. ARE YOU LOOKING FOR A LOST BLACK CAT WITH GREEN EYES? CALL 343-5515, EVENINGS.

For two evenings, nobody calls. On the third evening, the telephone rings. A woman tells Lucky she is looking for her black cat, who is lost. Lucky gives her directions to come to his apartment. Maybe Unlucky belongs to her.

The woman's name is Alice. She is small, about thirty-five years old. She is not beautiful, but she has a nice face and a soft voice.

"Yes, that's my cat!" she cries. "How can I ever thank you for finding her?"

She explains that her husband is dead and she has no children. Her life is lonely without her cat.

"I can see that you like my cat too," Alice says. "I hate to take her away from you. Please come and visit us soon. Come tomorrow. I'm a good cook. I am going to cook a chicken dinner for all three of us."

Lucky promises to come.

That night he thinks about Alice. He likes her. He wants to know her better. He remembers the fortune in the fortune cookie. He suddenly remembers the diamond ring, too.

"Is Unlucky going to bring me good luck?" he wonders.

Exercises

I.   Vocabulary

You probably know many of these words from reading the story and looking at the pictures. If there are still some you don't know, look them up in your dictionary now.

find	ring	lonely	sand
suppose(d) to	remember	beach	belong (to)
promise	advertisement (ad)		

II.   Definitions

Try to guess the best definition for these words. Then look then up in your dictionary and draw a circle around the answer.

1. to find
    a. to discover
    b. to feel
    c. to hold

2. suppose(d) to
    a. to be sure to
    b. to be compare(d) to
    c. to be believe(d)

3. belong (to)
    a. to be owned
    b. to be long
    c. to be like

4. to promise
    a. to refuse
    b. to agree
    c. to ask

5. lonely
    a. separate
    b. together
    c. crowded

6. remember
    a. wait for
    b. think back
    c. look for

III. Reading Comprehension

Read the questions. Find the answers in the story. Write the answers under the questions.

1. Why do Luis Lopez's friends call him "Lucky"?

   _____

   _____

2. When nobody calls to ask about the ring in Lucky's ad, what does he do with it?

   _____

   _____

3. What does the fortune cookie tell Lucky?

   _____

   _____

4. Why does Lucky call the cat "Unlucky"?

   _____

   _____

5. Why is Alice glad to get her cat?

   _____

   _____

6. Why does Alice ask Lucky to come for dinner?

   _____

   _____

IV. Discussion
Look at the pictures. Talk to your partner. Use words from the story.

Picture #1
Where is Lucky? What does the
waiter bring him?
Does he feel lucky?

Picture #2
What is Alice telling Lucky?
How does she thank him for finding
her cat?

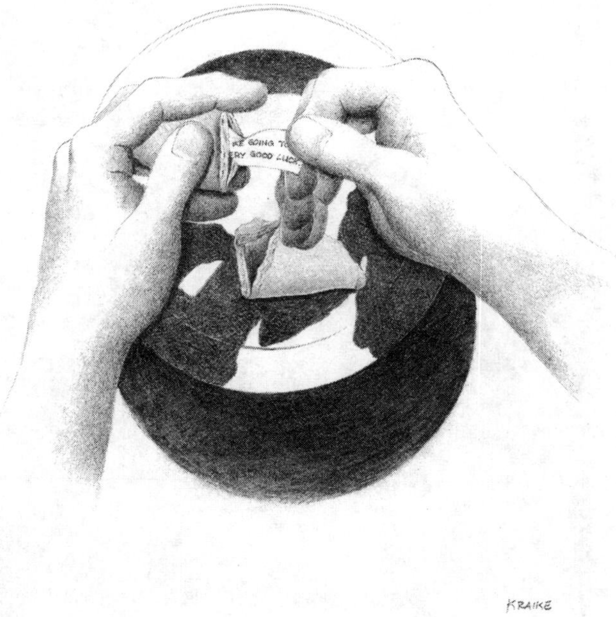

V. Writing
Write four things that Luis Lopez finds or that happen to him to make him seem
lucky.

1. _____

2. _____

3. _____

4. _____

"Wait until you hear the news."

A Double Chocolate Ice Cream Cone

Plum, North Dakota, is a very small town. It has one drugstore, one barber shop, one beauty shop and one little bank. Every Friday, a few of the working women of Plum eat lunch together at the drugstore. The sandwiches are good and the ice cream is delicious.

"Nothing exciting ever happens in Plum," complains Carol Webb at the Friday lunch. Carol works in the beauty shop. She says exactly the same thing every Friday.

"Plum bores me," Lisa Lee says, and turns a page of her book. Lisa works in the bank. She always reads during the Friday lunches to show that the conversation of the other women does not interest her.

"Oh, Lisa, why do you always act as if you're better than everybody else?" asks Janet Zabrowsky. Janet works in the bank, too.

Lisa doesn't answer. She just goes on reading.

The next Friday, Janet arrives late. She runs into the drugstore out of breath. Her eyes shine with excitement.

"Wait until you hear the news," she cries. "You are not going to believe it. I can't believe it myself. Things like this never happen in Plum!"

"Things like what?" asks Carol. "Come on, tell us!"

"I have to catch my breath first. Listen, they're going to make a movie, right here in Plum! A big Hollywood movie company is coming in August. And that's not all. I'm saving the best part for last. Can you guess who is going to be the star of this movie?"

Carol shakes her head. No, she can't guess. Lisa doesn't want to guess. Movie actors bore her.

"It's…Gregory Gordon," Janet whispers.

Gregory Gordon is famous for his bright blue eyes, coal black hair and beautiful, deep voice. He is one of the most popular actors in the world.

"Gregory Gordon is coming to Plum!" cries Carol. "It's too good to be true. Maybe we can see him. Maybe we can even talk to him. Oh, Lisa, if I meet him on the street and he says good morning to me, I'm afraid I'm going to faint."

"I'm not," says Lisa coldly. "I don't get excited about movie stars, not even Gregory Gordon."

In August, the movie company arrives with big trucks and many lights and cameras and dozens of busy people. Everyone in the town of Plum watches them shoot a scene in front of the barbershop. Everyone but Lisa. Everyone in town sees Gregory Gordon taking a walk on a hot evening, just like ordinary people. Everyone but Lisa. She has better things to do, she says.

The weather continues to be hot. One afternoon, Lisa leaves the bank and goes to the drugstore for ice cream.

"A double chocolate ice cream cone," she tells the boy at the counter. She takes a dollar out of her purse to pay. It falls out of her hand. The man waiting behind her picks it up.

"I think this is your dollar," says a deep, famous voice.

Lisa turns around and sees those bright blue eyes, the coal black hair, and that white, wonderful smile.

"Thank you very much," she whispers to Gregory Gordon.

Then she turns right around and doesn't look at him again. Her hands are shaking, her face is hot, her feet are cold, and her heart is beating one hundred and thirty times a minute.

"I hope he can't hear my heart," she thinks. "I am not going to let him see that I am excited. I am going to act as if nothing special is happening. I am going to act as if I don't even notice him. I hope I am not going to faint."

Lisa pays for her ice cream. The boy gives her a double chocolate cone and fifteen cents change. She tries not to look at Gregory Gordon, although he seems to be looking at her rather strangely. Lisa leaves the store. She finds herself out on the sidewalk feeling confused. Why is she holding fifteen cents in her hand instead of an ice cream cone? Lisa returns to the drugstore.

She asks the boy, "Where is my ice cream cone?"

"I give up," he says. "Where is it?"

Gregory Gordon touches Lisa on the shoulder. "Your ice cream cone is in your purse," he says. And he gives her a big, white, wonderful smile.

Exercises

I. Vocabulary
You probably know many of these words from reading the story and looking at the pictures. If there are still some you don't know, look them up in your dictionary now.

complain	bore	shoulder	breath
notice	guess	coal	whisper
famous	deep	confused	voice
faint	touch		

II. Definitions
Try to guess the best definition for these words. Then look them up in your dictionary and draw a circle around the answer.

1. breath
    a. a cool drink
    b. air you take in
    c. bright idea in your brain

2. coal (black hair)
    a. chocolate flavor
    b. color of the sea
    c. dark as night

3. deep (voice)
    a. loud
    b. musical
    c. low

4. faint
    a. fall down unconscious
    b. get a headache
    c. disappear

5. famous
    a. has great knowledge
    b. is unknown
    c. is well known

6. confused
    a. mixed up
    b. disturbed
    c. embarrassed

III. Reading Comprehension
Read the questions. Find the answers to the story. Write the answers under the questions.

1. How does Lisa show that the conversation of the other women does not interest her?

   _____

   _____

2. What is Gregory Gordon famous for?

   _____

   _____

3. What arrives in Plum in August?

   _____

   _____

4. How does Lisa feel after Gregory Gordon gives her the dollar she drops?

   _____

   _____

5. What does Lisa try not to do?

   _____

   _____

6. Where does Gregory Gordon tell Lisa to look for her ice cream cone?

   _____

   _____

IV. Discussion

Look at the pictures. Talk to your partner. Use words from the story.

Picture #1.
What is happening here?
How does Lisa feel?
How does she act?

Picture #2.
Lisa is asking for her ice cream cone.
Who knows where it is?
What do you think Lisa says when
she finds out?

V. Writing

Dictation. Study the first paragraph in the story for a few minutes. Think about
spelling and punctuation. Then close your book and write as the teacher dictates.
When you finish, open your book and check your work. Correct your mistakes.

"One more pull is going to do it."

Baby Flies Away

The Sullivan family is planning to move to a new house. Mr. and Mrs. Sullivan and their little boy, Andy, are excited about moving. They are also worried. How is Baby going to like living in a different house?

Baby is the Sullivans' three month old cat. She is all white except for green eyes, gray ears and a gray tail. The Sullivans love Baby, especially Andy.

"I hope Baby doesn't decide to run away from our new house," Mrs. Sullivan worries. She asks her friends for advice. What is the best way to move a cat?

"When you get to your new house, keep your cat inside for a week," one friend says. "Don't let her go out!"

"Give your cat little pieces of aspirin to make her sleepy," says another friend.

"After you move a cat to a new home, always put butter on its paws," advises a third friend. She doesn't say why.

Moving day arrives. All the beds and chairs and tables go to the new house in a moving truck. Baby travels to the new house in the car with the family. The little cat hates the car. She cries all the way.

At the new house, Mrs. Sullivan makes sure Baby stays inside. Andy stays in with her to keep her company. Every night, Mr. Sullivan gives Baby a tiny piece of aspirin. Every morning, Mrs. Sullivan puts butter on Baby's paws.

After a week it is time to let Baby out of the house.

"Do you think it's all right?" worries Mrs. Sullivan.

"Nothing bad can happen," says Mr. Sullivan. "We are all going out with her."

Baby walks around the yard slowly and carefully. She smells the fence. She smells the grass. She smells every flower. She sees a butterfly and tries to catch it.

"I think Baby likes her new home," say Andy.

Just then a big, black dog runs into the yard. He's a friendly dog but Baby doesn't know that. Up a tree she goes. Up, up, up she goes to the very top. There she hangs on, crying. No matter what the Sullivans do, Baby won't come down.

The tree is tall but young. The branches are too thin for Mr. Sullivan to climb.

"Call the Fire Department and ask them to bring a ladder!" he tells his wife.

The Fire Department is sorry. They don't rescue cats out of trees anymore.

"Daddy, you have to do something!" cries Andy.

"I'm thinking, I'm thinking," Mr. Sullivan says. "Wait, I know what to do. There is a long rope in the garage..."

Mr. Sullivan throws the rope over the tree. He hopes to pull the top of the tree down low. When it is low enough, he plans to reach Baby and rescue her. He pulls and pulls. Mrs. Sullivan helps him pull. Andy helps too. The tree bends lower, lower. Baby is now almost within reach.

"One more pull is going to do it," calls Mr. Sullivan.

They all pull as hard as they can. All of a sudden the rope breaks. The top of the tree whips back fast. Baby goes flying through the air. Up she flies over the fence, over the roof, out of sight.

All that week the Sullivans look for their cat. They look in as many places as they possibly can. They put signs in store windows offering $100 reward. No one calls. Baby seems to be gone forever. After a month of looking and of feeling very sad, the Sullivans get a new little cat. In time, they all learn to love the new cat.

A year passes. The Sullivans begin to make new friends. One of their neighbors, Mrs. Rose, invites them to dinner. Mr. and Mrs. Rose live near the Sullivans, but on a different street.

The first thing Andy notices at the Roses' house is their big, beautiful cat. She is a white cat with green eyes, gray ears and a gray tail.

"Why, that's Baby!" Andy cries.

Mrs. Rose picks up the cat and kisses her on her pink nose. "Her name is Angel," she tells Andy. "Let me explain. One afternoon during the summer, my husband is sitting in the yard reading. Suddenly a small white cat flies through the air from nowhere. She lands right in the middle of his newspaper. We call her "Angel' because she comes directly from heaven." Mrs. Rose is smiling. It's hard to know if she is joking or not.

Mr. and Mrs. Sullivan look at each other. Mr. Sullivan says, "That's a very interesting story. And we have one to tell you, too..."

Exercises

I. Vocabulary

You probably know many of these words from reading the story and looking at the pictures. If there are still some you don't know, look them up in your dictionary now.

excited	advice	branch	bend
joke (joking)	move	hate	climb
sign	heaven	decide	worry (worries)
rescue	sad		

II. Definitions

Try to guess the best definition for these words. Then look them up in your dictionary and draw a circle around the best answer.

1. excited
   a. tired
   b. eager
   c. disappointed

2. advice
   a. an order
   b. a law
   c. a suggestion

3. hate
   a. dislike
   b. enjoy
   c. expect

4. branch
   a. a limb
   b. a piece
   c. a part

5. rescue
   a. remove
   b. hold
   c. save

6. joking
   a. talking
   b. being polite
   c. telling a funny story

35

III. Reading Comprehension

Read the questions. Find the answers in the story. Write the answers under the questions.

1. How does Baby travel to the new house?

    _____

    _____

2. What does Baby do when she sees a big dog in the yard?

    _____

    _____

3. How does Mr. Sullivan plan to reach Baby and rescue her?

    _____

    _____

4. What happens when the tree whips back?

    _____

    _____

5. What is the first thing Andy notices at the Roses' house?

    _____

    _____

6. Why does the Roses' cat have the name "Angel"?

    _____

    _____

IV. Discussion

Look at the pictures. Talk to your partner. Use words from the story.

Picture #1.
Why is Andy holding Baby in the car?
Where is Baby going to stay for the first week in the new house? What are the Sullivans going to do to keep Baby from running away?

Picture #2
What does Andy say when he sees the Roses' cat?
Why does he think the cat is Baby?
What interesting story is Mr. Sullivan going to tell the Rose family about Angel?

V. Writing

What things go to the new house in the moving truck?

_____

_____

Baby climbs up a tree, and Mr. Sullivan can't get her. Why?

_____

_____

After Baby flies away, what do the Sullivans do to try to find her?

_____

_____

"Good morning, honey. You sound different."

Mother and Daughter
A Play

THE CHARACTERS: Mother, about fifty years old.

                                  Julie, about twenty-five years old.

Julie: Hello?

Mother: Good morning, honey. You sound different. You don't sound like yourself.

Julie: That's because I have a terrible cold. My throat hurts and even my ears hurt. Oh, Mom, I want to stay in bed today, but I can't. I have to go to the market.

Mother: No you don't! It's raining. You don't want to take the baby out in the rain, do you?

Julie: I don't want to, but I have to. There's nothing in the refrigerator. There's nothing for dinner. I don't have enough food for the baby. Oh, my throat really hurts! (She coughs.)

Mother: I can go to the market for you.

Julie: I hate to ask you, Mom. It's raining so hard...

Mother: Who's afraid of a little rain? I'm coming. I'm coming on the 11:20 bus. I know you need baby food. What else do you need?

Julie: Please buy milk, two quarts. And a dozen eggs. Three grapefruit. Six oranges. A can of coffee. A large can of tomatoes. Four or five green apples and two red apples. Three bananas. Two pounds of onions. A chicken. A bottle of cooking oil. A jar of strawberry jelly. Six cans of

39

	dog food and some paper towels. Is that too much for you to carry in the rain, Mom?
Mother:	For a mother, nothing is too much. When I come to your house, you can get into your nice, warm bed and sleep all day. Don't worry about the baby. I know how to take care of babies.
Julie:	The baby loves you, Mom. And so do I. And so does David.
Mother:	I'm glad you love me. I'm glad the baby loves me. I'm glad David loves me—who's David?
Julie:	Mom, what's the matter with you? Don't you know David, my husband, the father of your only grandson?
Mother:	I don't have a grandson. I have a granddaughter. Susan, your voice sounds very strange. It doesn't sound like you at all. Are you sure it is you?
Julie:	Mother, are you all right? You are frightening me. I'm your daughter Julie!
Mother:	Oh, this is a terrible mistake! I should never call anybody on the telephone without first putting on my glasses. This is a wrong number! My daughter's name is Susan, not Julie. I'm very sorry, but you are not my daughter and I am not your mother. Please excuse me. I hope you feel better tomorrow. Good-bye. (She hangs up.)
Julie:	(very disappointed) Oh, no...does that mean she's not coming?

Exercises

I. Vocabulary
You probably know many of these words from reading the story and looking at the pictures. If there are still some you don't know, look them up in your dictionary now.

state	grapefruit	chicken	throat
eggs	oil	cough	orange
jelly	hate	apple	worry
dozen	banana	frighten	tomatoes
onion	mistake		

II. Definitions
Try to guess the best definition for these words. Then look them up in your dictionary and draw a circle around the answer.

1. stage
    a. a stack of dishes in the sink
    b. a place to keep horses
    c. a place for actors at the theater

2. throat
    a. the front part of your neck
    b. the inside of your hand
    c. the first finger

3. to hate
    a. to have pain
    b. to be unhappy
    c. not to like

4. worry
    a. feel warm
    b. feel uneasy
    c. feel like working

5. to frighten
    a. to make afraid
    b. to get dressed
    c. to become very cold

6. mistake
    a. a misunderstanding
    b. an error
    c. an accident

III. Reading Comprehension
Read the questions. Find the answers in the story. Write the answers under the questions.

1. What is Mother doing in her apartment?

   _____

   _____

2. Why does Julie say she sounds different?

   _____

   _____

3. What does Mother say she can do for her daughter?

   _____

   _____

4. Is it too much for Mother to carry all the food?

   _____

   _____

5. Does Mother have a grandson?

   _____

   _____

6. What should Mother do before calling anybody on the telephone?

   _____

   _____

IV. Discussion
Look at the pictures. Talk to your partner. Use
words from the story.

Picture 1.
How does she feel?
What hurts her?
Why does she need to go out in the rain?

Picture #2.
What is Mother going to buy for her daughter
at the market?
Does Mother have a daughter named Julie?
Does Mother have a granddaughter?
What does she have?
Does Julie have a son or a daughter?
Is Mother going to go to the market? Why?

V. Writing
Write three reasons why Julie feels bad.

1. _____

2. _____

3. _____

What does Mother want her daughter to do when she comes to her house?

_____

_____

"Now the cow is safe," thinks Laszlo.

A Woman's Work
(An Old Folk Tale)

Far, far away, on the other side of the world, live a farmer and his wife. Their small house leans against the side of a hill. Earth covers the roof of the house. Green grass and little yellow flowers grow on it.

Laszlo, the farmer, works hard. He digs the soil. He plants corn and wheat. He cuts the hay. There is always too much to do. After dinner, he likes to rest and smoke his pipe. If his wife, Maruska, asks him to hold the baby, or to feed the chickens, he smiles and shakes his head no.

"My work is hard," Laszlo reminds Maruska, "and your work is easy. What do you do all day? You cook a little. You clean a little. You take care of one child, one cow and a few chickens. A woman's work is easy, Maruska."

"Oh, do you really think so?" Maruska says. "All right, tomorrow let us change jobs. I'm going out to the field to do your work. You can stay home to do mine."

Laszlo laughs and agrees.

Long before the sun comes up the next day, Maruska goes off to the field. Laszlo stays in bed until he feels hungry. Then he gets up to cook breakfast. "This is an easy life," he tells himself. While his breakfast is cooking in the fireplace, the baby, Katya, wakes up. He goes to dress her and forgets his breakfast. It burns. Just then, the cow begins to moo and cry. Laszlo remembers it is time to milk her. But he is still hungry. He finds another pan and starts to cook breakfast all over again. Then he takes Katya to the barn so he can watch her while he milks the cow. The cow gives a big pail full of milk. Laszlo is happy about that—until he smells something. It is his breakfast burning for the second time. He runs to the kitchen and takes the pan off the fire. When he gets back to the barn he finds the pail of milk lying on its side. All the milk is gone. Katya is wet with milk from her head to her toes.

"Oh, you bad little Katya," says Laszlo. He decides to take her with him to the garden to pick vegetables. He is going to cook a delicious vegetable soup for dinner. While he is filling big baskets with tomatoes and onions, carrots and potatoes, he hears the cow crying again.

The cow is hungry. Laszlo feels bad for not remembering to take her to a little field where she always eats the grass. Now it is too late to take her there. Instead, Laszlo leads her up the hill to the roof of the house. She can eat the good green grass that grows there.

Back in the kitchen, the farmer puts a great big pot of water in the fireplace. He is ready to cook the soup. He starts to peel the vegetables. He peels so hard and so fast that he forgets to light the fire under the pot. (Which turns out to be a good thing, as we are soon going to learn.)

Now Laszlo is worrying about the cow on the roof. He is afraid she may fall off and break her leg. So he gets a long rope. He ties one end around the cow's middle. Then he throws the other end down the chimney, through the fireplace and into the kitchen. There, Laszlo ties the rope tightly around himself. "Now the cow is safe," thinks Laszlo. He continues peeling the vegetables.

The cow sees some grass she especially wants right at the very edge of the roof. She moves closer and closer to it and...falls! Now the cow is hanging low against the side of the house. Her weight on the rope pulls Laszlo half way up the chimney. He can not move farther up or farther down.

He calls as loudly as he can. Nobody hears him except Katya who thinks it is a game and laughs.

At the end of the day, Maruska comes home from the field. She is a little tired, but she is whistling a happy song. The first thing she sees is the cow hanging by its middle against the side of the house. The poor animal is almost dead. Maruska quickly gets a knife and cuts the rope. Down comes the cow onto the flowers below. At the same time, Laszlo falls down the chimney right into the big pot of water. That is where his wife finds him.

Maruska looks around the kitchen. Her husband is sitting in a pot of water. Her child is on the floor with vegetable peel in her hair. There is vegetable peel everywhere. There are enough peeled vegetables for the whole town. There are two burned pans waiting for someone to wash them.

"Well, husband," she says, "do you still think my work is easier than yours?"

Laszlo lifts himself out of the water. "Your work is harder, much harder," he admits.

"Then please feed the chickens while I wash the baby," Maruska asks.

Laszlo does, gladly.

Exercises

I. Vocabulary

You probably know many of these words from reading the story and looking at the pictures. If there are still some you don't know, look them up in your dictionary now.

dig   burn   hang   plant
barn   peel   field   pail
rope   forget   climb   admit
soil

II. Definitions

Try to guess the best definition for these words. Then look them up in your dictionary and draw a circle around the answer.

1. to plant
   - a. to break up the ground
   - b. to put into soil
   - c. to turn up earth

2. field
   - a. a piece of land
   - b. a neighborhood
   - c. a forest

3. climb
   - a. go down
   - b. jump up
   - c. go up

4. to hang
   - a. to support
   - b. to stay
   - c. to stand

5. rope
   - a. a strong cord
   - b. a thin hair
   - c. a long belt

6. admit
   - a. to be right
   - b. to disagree
   - c. to say (something) is true

47

III. Reading Comprehension

Read the questions. Find the answers in the story. Write the answers under the questions.

1. What is growing on the roof of the small house?

   _____

   _____

2. Why doesn't Laszlo help Maruska? What does he say about their work?

   _____

   _____

3. After his breakfast burns for the second time, Laszlo comes back to the barn. Where is the milk? What is the matter with Katya?

   _____

   _____

4. Why does Laszlo take the hungry cow up to the roof of the house?

   _____

   _____

5. Why does Laszlo tie the rope around the cow?

   _____

   _____

6. Laszlo ties the other end of the rope around himself. What happens to him when the cow falls off the roof?

   _____

   _____

7. What happens to Laszlo when Maruska cuts the rope?

   _____

   _____

IV. Discussion

Look at the pictures. Talk to your partner.
Use words from the story.

Picture #1.
Where is
Maruska
going? Why is
she doing this?

Picture #2.
Why is the baby laughing?
Why is Laszlo in the pot?
Does he now think a man's work is easier than a
woman's work?

V. Writing

Write three things you know about the farmer's house.

1. _____

2. _____

3. _____

Write three things you know about Laszlo's work.

1. _____

2. _____

3. _____

Write three things Maruska does every day.

1. _____

2. _____

3. _____

"Take off your mask, friend, and let me see who you are."

The Appointment

Every November 2, Latin Americans celebrate "The Day of the Dead." In Mexico, especially, it is a happy holiday. It is happy not only for the living, but also for the dead. Many people believe that on this day the dead come back to earth to visit their families. In honor of the day, stores sell cakes and candies in the form of Death. Some people wear paper masks that look like Death's ugly face. Everyone enjoys this fiesta, or holiday.

In the little Mexican town of San Cristobal live a rich man, Señor Esteban, and his handsome young servant, Emilio. Señor Esteban is very old and can no longer walk without a walking stick. Emilio cooks for him and takes care of him.

On November 2, "The Day of the Dead," Señor Esteban decides he wants to eat a piece of fish for his dinner. He asks Emilio to go to the market to buy fish. The market place is very crowded. It is late afternoon. Excited children dance around small fires that are burning at every street corner. Most of the people of the town are in the market place. They are talking, visiting, enjoying the thousands of candles and flowers. Many of them are wearing paper masks that look like the face of Death. One man wearing such a mask seems to be very interested in Emilio. He keeps looking at him.

"Maybe I know him," thinks Emilio. He walks over to the man in the mask and tells him cheerfully, "Take off your mask, friend, and let me see who you are."

"I really don't wish to do that yet," replies the man in a strange voice.

"Don't be that way," says Emilio. "Come on, take it off."

"If you insist," says the man, "but you are going to see my face again soon enough." He removes the paper mask. Under it is the terrible, bone-white face of Death.

Emilio's heart begins to beat so fast that he fears it will stop altogether. He runs home as quickly as he can. He tells Señor Esteban about meeting Death in the market place.

"Help me," Emilio begs Señor Esteban. "I am too young to die."

"How can I help you?" the old man asks.

"Give me some money. I will take the bus to Puebla. I can be there in four hours. Puebla is a big city. I can hide there. I can surely escape Death there."

Señor Esteban gladly gives Emilio more than enough money. The servant does not even take the time to pack a shirt or a toothbrush. He hurries to catch the bus, and soon he is on his way to Puebla.

In the evening, the old man remembers that he wants to eat fish for dinner. He takes his walking stick and slowly walks to the market place. It is still very crowded, but he recognizes Death immediately.

"Good evening, Señor Death," Señor Esteban calls. "I hope you are here in San Cristobal for me."

"No, not for you. Not yet," Death replies kindly.

"Why not?" the old man asks. "My legs are almost useless. I have no teeth to eat with. I am lonely because all my friends are dead. Why can't you take me? Surely it is time for me to die."

"I am sorry, it is not time yet," says Death.

"Are you here in San Cristobal because of my servant, Emilio?" Señor Esteban asks. "Why Emilio and not me? He is so young. He is still afraid to die."

Death answers, "Today I am not here in San Cristobal to get either you or Emilio. I have an appointment with someone else. Meeting Emilio this afternoon in the market place is as much a surprise to me as to him."

"A surprise?" asks Señor Esteban. "Why is it a surprise?"

"Because," says Death, "I have an appointment with Emilio late tonight, in Puebla."

Exercises

I. Vocabulary

You probably know many of these words from reading the story and looking at the pictures. If there are still some you don't know, look them up in your dictionary now.

appointment	mask	beg	dead
ugly	hurry (hurries)	honor	decide
recognize	form	crowded	

II. Definitions

Try to guess the best definition for these words. Then look them up in your dictionary and draw a circle around the answer.

1. appointment
   a. a greeting
   b. a date
   c. a fight

2. (in) honor (of)
   a. with respect for
   b. in favor of
   c. in exchange for

3. form
   a. fashion
   b. model
   c. shape

4. decide (to)
   a. refuse to
   b. to have to
   c. make up your mind to

5. beg
   a. to ask
   b. to agree
   c. to allow

6. recognize
   a. know
   b. find
   c. get

III. Reading Comprehension

Read the questions. Find the answers in the story. Write the answers under the questions.

1. Why is "The Day of the Dead" a happy holiday for many people?

   _____

   _____

2. When Emilio sees a man wearing a Death mask looking at him, what does he say?

   _____

   _____

3. What reasons does Emilio have for going to Puebla? What does he say?

   _____

   _____

4. Why doesn't Death take Old Señor Esteban now?

   _____

   _____

5. Why is Death here in San Cristobal this day?

   _____

   _____

6. Why is the meeting with Emilio a surprise for Death?

   _____

   _____

IV. Discussion

Look at the pictures. Talk to your partner. Use words from the story.

Picture #1.
What does Emilio want?
Where is he going to go?
Why does he think he is going to be safe?

Picture #2.
What is Señor Esteban telling Death about himself?
Why is Death in San Cristobal?
What is Death going to do late tonight?

V. Writing

Dictation. Study the second paragraph in the story for a few minutes. Think about spelling and punctuation. Then close your book and write as the teacher dictates. When you finish, open your book and check your work. Correct your mistakes.

_____

_____

_____

_____

_____

The Rajah's servant tries to explain to the men that
each of them is right and also wrong.

The Blind Men and the Elephant
(Adapted from a folk tale)

There is a forest in India where the trees grow very tall. Birds with bright feathers live in these trees. Monkeys swing from branch to branch. Under the tall trees is a village with a few small houses. The smallest belongs to six men who live there together. All six are blind.

They are blind, but they are happy. Life is good to them. They like each other and help each other. When one washes the clothes, another hangs them up to dry. When one bakes the bread, another cooks the vegetables for dinner. During the day, they all work in the garden. At night, they sit around the warm stove and talk in quiet voices. No one ever hears the sound of a quarrel in the house of the six blind men.

There is exciting news. The Rajah, or prince, is returning to his great summer house near the village. He is bringing his wife and children, his sisters and brothers and cousins, his cooks and servants and gardeners. And of course, the Rajah never goes anywhere without his famous elephant, Ravi. Ravi is the biggest, tallest, most beautiful elephant in all of India.

The whole village is excited and the six blind men are excited too. They are especially excited about the elephant. They can't imagine what an elephant is like. They all want a chance to find out.

The Rajah hears about the six blind men. He hears that they want to learn what an elephant is like. The Rajah kindly sends one of his servants to lead the six friends to his house. The servant immediately brings them to the yard where Ravi is tied. At last they are going to understand! They agree to take turns. One at a time, they feel Ravi with their hands to discover what he looks like.

The first blind man happens to touch the side of the great elephant's body. "Now I know what an elephant is," he says. "An elephant is like a wall."

The second blind man happens to touch the point of Ravi's tusk. The tusks are the two long teeth that stick out of an elephant's mouth. The point of a tusk is very sharp.

"Now I know what an elephant is," the second blind man says. "An elephant is like a sword."

The third blind man happens to touch one of the elephant's tall, wide legs.

"Now I know what an elephant is," he says. "An elephant is like a tree."

The fourth blind man happens to touch the elephant's short, thin tail.

"Now I know what an elephant is," he says. "An elephant is like a piece of rope."

The fifth blind man happens to touch the elephant's ear.

"Now I know what an elephant is," the fifth blind man says. "An elephant is like a fan. It is like the fans we use to cool ourselves on hot summer days."

The sixth blind man happens to touch the elephant's trunk. "An elephant is nothing like a fan, or a rope, or a wall," he says. "It is like a big, fat snake."

The Rajah's servant tries to explain to the men that each of them is right and also wrong. He tries to tell them that an elephant is like all the things they describe. But they are too busy quarreling to listen.

Every one of the six blind men is sure that only he is right and that the others are wrong. They argue all the way to their village. That night, there is the sound of loud, angry voices in the house of the six blind men. The next day, when the third blind man washes the clothes, none of the others wants to hang them up to dry. When the fifth blind man bakes bread, the first blind man refuses to cook the vegetables for dinner.

"I don't want to cook for a fool who thinks an elephant is like a fan," he says. "Any child can tell you that an elephant is exactly like a wall."

Weeks, months and years go by. The blind men quarrel most of the day. They quarrel most of the night. And they are probably quarreling at this very minute.

Exercises

I. Vocabulary

You probably know many of these words from reading the story and looking at the pictures. If there are still some you don't know, look them up in your dictionary now.

blind	quarrel	wall	village
elephant	sword	stove	imagine
fan	monkey	touch	rope
snake			

II. Definitions

Try to guess the best definitions for these words. Then look them up in your dictionary and draw a circle around the answer.

1. blind
   - a. cannot sit
   - b. cannot stand
   - c. cannot see

2. quarrel
   - a. question
   - b. disagreement
   - c. disappointment

3. village
   - a. a small town
   - b. a large island
   - c. a tall tree

4. imagine
   - a. know
   - b. guess
   - c. understand

5. touch
   - a. feel
   - b. forget
   - c. frighten

6. sword
   - a. a bed spring
   - b. a blank check
   - c. a knife blade

III. Reading Comprehension

Read the questions. Find the answers in the story. Write the answers under the questions.

1. Why are the six blind men happy?

   _____

   _____

2. Why is everyone especially excited?

   _____

   _____

3. What do the blind men do to understand how an elephant looks?

   _____

   _____

4. Why can't the Rajah's servant explain to the men that each one is right and also wrong?

   _____

   _____

5. Why do the blind men argue all the way back to the village?

   _____

   _____

6. What are the blind men probably doing now?

   _____

   _____

IV. Discussion

Look at the pictures. Talk to your partner. Use words from the story.

Picture #1.
What different parts of the elephant do the blind men touch? What do they think each part is like?

Picture #2.
What is the Rajah's servant saying to the blind men?

V. Writing

Write what part of the elephant each blind man touches, and what he believes it is.

_____

_____

_____

_____

_____

_____

What kind of a lesson can we learn from this story?

_____

_____

_____

"Get out of the rain, girl."

MaryJo Gets a Ride Home
(Adapted from an Urban Legend)

Barney Baker is a truck driver. He delivers refrigerators from a factory in Ohio to stores in Florida. It is 1936, and good jobs are hard to find. Barney is an excellent driver and he likes his job. Tonight, though, it is raining so hard that he can hardly see the road. It is late and he is tired. When he finds a coffee shop that is still open, he goes in. He parks his big, long truck and runs through the rain to the coffee shop door.

Near the door there is a girl, about fourteen years old, Barney thinks, sitting on a bench. She is wearing only a blue skirt, a white blouse, and dirty white shoes. Her clothes and her hair are as wet as they can be. She doesn't seem to notice.

Barney has two daughters of his own. He wonders why this girl is sitting here, all alone, on such a wet night.

"Get out of the rain, girl!" he calls to her as he runs into the coffee shop.

Barney orders coffee, a piece of lemon pie, and more coffee. A half hour passes before he is ready to leave.

The girl is still sitting on the bench. She looks even wetter and colder than before. Barney starts to walk past her, but can't do it.

"Are you in some kind of trouble?" he asks her.

She says nothing.

"It's late. Why aren't you home, in bed?"

Again, she says nothing.

"Listen," Barney tells her, "I'm trying to help you. What's your name? How old are you?"

"MaryJo. MaryJo Haggarty," the girl whispers. "I'm eighteen years old."

The look on Barney's face shows he doesn't believe her.

"I really am eighteen," the girl says. "Today is my birthday. If I can only get home, my mother probably has a birthday cake for me, with eighteen candles."

"Where's your home?" Barney wants to know.

"In Allenburg, just six miles down the road. It's a yellow house, across the street from the church. Please, Mister, can you drive me there?"

Barney looks at his watch. He's already late. "No, but I can give you five cents to phone home."

The girl shakes her long, wet hair. "That doesn't work. I try and try to call them but they never answer. Please drive me, it isn't very far."

Barney imagines one of his own daughters out on a night like this. He tells MaryJo to get in the truck and he puts his warm jacket around her.

"Wear it," he says, "or you'll catch cold."

They drive on and on through the rain. Barney and MaryJo are both quiet. They don't have much to say to each other. Then Barney sees a big, dark building ahead.

"Is that the church near your house?" he asks.

MaryJo says it is. She thanks Barney for the ride and whispers that she wants to get out now.

"Wait. Let me open the door for you," says Barney.

He walks around to the other side of the truck and opens the door. MaryJo does not get out. Barney gets his flashlight and shines it all around. She is not in the truck. She is not near the truck. She is not anywhere. How can a person disappear like that? Can she be home, already?

Barney knocks on the door of the yellow house. A woman, MaryJo's mother, opens it. No, her daughter is not here, she says. She listens to Barney's story without much surprise.

"You aren't the first driver to offer to take MaryJo home," she explains. "It happens every year on this date. My poor girl tries so hard to come home on her birthday, but she never, never comes."

"Mrs. Haggarty, where is MaryJo now?" Barney asks. MaryJo's mother opens an umbrella and takes Barney across the street into the dark church-yard. She leads the way among the graves of the dead and stops in front of a white gravestone. Barney shines his flashlight on it and reads:

MaryJo Haggarty
1918-1932
May She Rest in Peace

The mother is crying quietly. "An automobile accident," she says, "four years ago, on her fourteenth birthday."

Barney notices that there is something hanging on the corner of MaryJo's gravestone. It is his jacket.

Exercises

I. Vocabulary
You probably know many of these words from reading the story and looking at the pictures. If there are still some you don't know, look them up in your dictionary now.

truck	notice	grave	factory
trouble	peace	often	flashlight
hang	wet	imagine	accident
bench	surprise		

II. Definitions
Try to guess a best definition for these words. Then look them up in your dictionary and draw a circle around the answer.

1. often
   a. once in a while
   b. many times
   c. sometimes

2. to notice
   a. to pay attention
   b. to know
   c. to be aware

3. (be in) trouble
   a. be displeased
   b. be unworried
   c. have problems

4. imagine
   a. to suppose
   b. to question
   c. to look through

5. surprise
   a. something unexpected
   b. doubt
   c. something certain

6. peace
   a. enjoyment
   b. quiet
   c. freedom

III. Reading Comprehension

Read the questions. Find the answers in the story. Write the answers under the questions.

1. Why is it so hard for Barney to drive tonight?

   _____

   _____

2. Why does MaryJo say she doesn't want to phone home?

   _____

   _____

3. Where is MaryJo when Barney drives her home and opens the door of the truck?

   _____

   _____

4. What does Mrs. Haggarty tell Barney about this date every year?

   _____

   _____

5. Where does Mrs. Haggarty lead Barney?

   _____

   _____

6. What does Barney notice in the graveyard?

   _____

   _____

IV. Discussion
Look at the pictures. Talk to your partner. Use words from the story.

Picture #1.
Where does MaryJo tell Barney she lives?
What special day is it for her?
How old is she?
What does she say is waiting for her at home?

Picture #2.
Is Mrs. Haggarty surprised at Barney's story?
What does she do to answer Barney's questions?
What do they see in the graveyard?

V. Writing
Dictation. Study the second paragraph in the story for a few minutes. Think about spelling and punctuation. Then close your book and write as the teacher dictates. When you finish, open your book and check your work. Correct your mistakes.

_____

_____

_____

_____

_____

_____

"This may hurt a little."

Androcles and the Lion
(Adapted from an Old Fable)

This is a story of long, long ago...

In the land of Egypt lives a slave named Androcles. He belongs to Antonius, an officer in the Roman army. At this time, the powerful armies of the Roman Emperor rule Egypt and also many other countries of the world.

Antonius makes Androcles work hard night and day. Poor Androcles is not strong or brave. He is a small, thin man who only wants to stay out of trouble. But his life is so unhappy that he sometimes thinks about running away. Maybe he can hide in a big city where Antonius can't find him.

One day, seven camels and their camel drivers pass by. Androcles hears the men talking. They say they are going to cross the great desert on their way to a big city.

"This is my chance," Androcles thinks. He says good-bye to Kiri, Antonius' cat. She is his only friend. Then he hurries after the camel drivers because they know the way to the big city. He is careful not to let the drivers see him. He is afraid they may catch him and send him back to Antonius.

From a safe distance, Androcles does exactly as the camel drivers do. They sleep during the heat of the day and travel in the cool of the night. He does the same. The only difference is that the drivers eat dinner every evening, and Androcles has nothing to eat. Being free isn't always easy. Poor Androcles tries to sleep a little longer while the men eat so he doesn't have to smell their rice and their meat.

Once, Androcles sleeps too long. When he wakes up, the camels and their drivers are already gone. He is all alone on the great desert.

"Oh, oh, what am I going to do now?" Androcles cries.

He walks this way. He walks that way. He comes to a place where the desert ends and the brown hills begin. Suddenly he hears a sound that turns his blood to ice. Sitting on one of the hills is a lion. He is a very large and very angry lion. Each of his paws is as big as a plate and his eyes burn like fire. When he opens his mouth, he roars, making a terrible sound that shakes the trees. Androcles runs away, as fast and far as he can.

He can still hear the lion, but now the roar sounds different. The lion sounds as if he is crying. He sounds like Kiri when something is hurting her. Curious, Androcles goes back. The lion doesn't seem interested in eating him. He is busy licking one of his paws with his tongue. Deep inside the paw is a splinter, a cruel needle of wood.

"You poor, dear lion," says Androcles who has a kind heart. Very slowly, very carefully, he walks up to the lion and gently examines his paw. The lion sits quietly and lets him do it.

"This may hurt a little," warns Androcles and pulls the splinter out. Feeling better now, the lion rubs his big head against Androcles. It is his way of saying thank you.

"Just like Kiri," Androcles thinks.

The lion takes Androcles to his cave. There the two live together happily for several days. The lion hunts and shares the meat with Androcles. At last the slave feels safe and free. But these good days come to an end. Some Roman soldiers march by. They catch the lion in a net. They put Androcles in chains. They send both the slave and the lion across the sea to Rome. There they lock Androcles in a stone prison. Where his dear lion is, he does not know.

It is the Roman custom to punish criminals, like runaway slaves, by making them fight lions in a big, round theater called an arena. This is very popular entertainment in Rome. The lion keepers at the arena do not feed the animals for many days before the fight. The audience enjoys seeing the hungry lions eat the criminals. Even the Emperor likes to watch.

The day comes when his guards take Androcles into the arena to fight a lion. The people laugh when they see the thin, weak little man shaking with fear. They think the lion will eat him in less than a minute.

The big iron gate opens and the lion rushes out, roaring. He is very hungry. He sees the man and understands he is finally getting his dinner. He intends to swallow this little man in just a few bites. Suddenly, when the lion is close to Androcles, he stops. He remembers him and begins to lick his face. Androcles puts his arms around the lion's neck and hugs his old friend. The audience doesn't believe what they are seeing. After the Emperor hears Androcles' story, he frees both the slave and the lion. He lets them return to Egypt together.

Exercises

I. Vocabulary

You probably know many of these words from reading the story and looking at the pictures. If there are still some you don't know, look them up in your dictionary now.

slave	distance	curious	prison
army	blood	paw	guard
rule	ice	net	swallow
thin	lion	chain	

II. Definitions

Try to guess the best definition for these words. Then look them up in your dictionary and draw a circle around the answer.

1. to rule
   a. to have success
   b. to have trouble
   c. to have control

2. thin
   a. slim
   b. slender
   c. skinny

3. distance
   a. a short time
   b. a long way
   c. a small space

4. curious
   a. interested
   b. careful
   c. forgetful

5. paw
   a. food
   b. fool
   c. foot

6. a guard
   a. a keeper
   b. a helper
   c. a partner

III. Reading Comprehension

Read the questions. Find the answers in the story. Write the answers under the questions.

1. What does Antonius want Androcles to do for him?

   _____

   _____

2. What does Androcles do when he first hears the lion roar?

   _____

   _____

3. What does Androcles do when he sees the splinter in the lion's paw?

   _____

   _____

4. What does the lion do for Androcles when they live together for several days?

   _____

   _____

5. Why don't the lion keepers feed the lions for many days before the fight?

   _____

   _____

6. What does the lion do when he is close to Androcles?

   _____

   _____

IV. Discussion

Look at the pictures. Talk to your partner. Use words from the story.

Picture #1.
Where do the Roman soldiers find Androcles and the lion?
What do they do to them?
Where do they send them?

Picture #2.
Where is Androcles?
How does the lion feel?
What happens when it comes close to Androcles?
What does the Emperor do after he hears Androcles' story?

V. Writing

Dictation. Study paragraph five. As you write, be careful about punctuation. Close your book as the teacher dictates. Then open your book and check your work.

_____

_____

_____

_____

_____

73

Jackie Robinson puts on the uniform of the famous Brooklyn Dodgers.

Jackie Robinson Plays Ball

Jackie Robinson is a star baseball, basketball and football player at the University of California. He becomes an "All American," a very great honor in sports in the United States. He is a hero in school. Everyone wants to be his friend.

When World War II begins, hundreds of thousands of young Americans are called to serve their country. Many African-Americans, black like Jackie Robinson, are called. A great number of them give their lives for their country. But black people still do not have the same rights or liberties as white people. Especially in the South. Jackie is educated, he is famous and he is popular. He becomes one of the few black officers in the United States Army. And it is to the South the army sends Jackie Robinson.

The qualities that make him a great sports hero soon get Jackie into trouble. In the South, blacks are supposed to sit in the back of the bus. He is insulted when a bus driver orders him to move to the back. Jackie refuses. The bus driver calls the military police. Jackie fights them. The army puts him on trial. He is found innocent, but he feels bitter when he leaves the army.

Since he is good at sports, Jackie becomes a professional baseball player. At this time, black teams play only against other black teams, and white teams play only against other white teams. Because of this separation, or segregation, black and white players never play together.

Jackie Robinson joins a black baseball team in Kansas City. They pay him $400 a month. He's good, he's very good, but he hates the life. He hates playing in Southern towns where restaurants don't serve him because he is black. Jackie is going to marry Rachel, a pretty, well-educated nurse. Maybe he should leave baseball altogether and find a better life for both of them.

Jackie doesn't know Branch Rickey, but he certainly knows his name. Rickey is the president of one of the most important white baseball clubs, the Brooklyn Dodgers. He is a religious person. He thinks it is wrong to keep a man out of a baseball team just because his skin is a different color. He sends someone to Kansas City to watch Jackie Robinson play. Then he invites Jack to come to his office in Brooklyn.

"Jack, I'm looking for a great colored ball player," Rickey says. "But I need more than a great player. I need a man who can accept insults. I need a man with the courage not to fight back. Can you do that?"

Jackie Robinson thinks for a long time before he answers. He knows that he is not good at accepting insults. But he also knows that the first black to play on a professional white baseball team needs special courage. He must never give anybody the excuse to say, "See? Mixing black and white players causes trouble." Jackie tells Rickey he can do it. Rickey hires Jackie to play for the Royals, a training team the Dodgers own.

The Royals do their spring training in Florida. Jackie and Rachel Robinson, just married, fly there from California. It's a journey they never forget. In New Orleans, they are put off the plane to make room for two white people. The next day, on another plane, the same thing happens. They finish their unhappy journey by bus.

During that first season with the Royals, Jackie works hard not to become angry. In one game, he makes a home run only to find a policeman waiting to arrest him at home plate. In Florida, they don't allow blacks to play ball with whites. What really hurts Jackie is that the rest of the team just stands there watching. Nobody defends him.

In 1947, there is an important meeting of baseball club owners. They discuss Branch Rickey's plan to bring Jackie Robinson to play with the Brooklyn Dodgers. Rickey is the only one who votes for the plan. He not only votes for it, he does it. In April, Jackie Robinson puts on the uniform of the famous Brooklyn Dodgers.

Maybe Brooklyn, part of New York City, is the perfect place for Rickey's experiment. There are three million Irish, Italians and Jews living in Brooklyn. Most of them are poor. Most of them are learning to live in peace with each other. Many of them love the Brooklyn Dodgers. As Robinson helps to win game after game for his team, bigger and bigger crowds attend the games. For the first time, many of the people buying tickets are black.

Still, players on other teams call him ugly names. They try to make him angry. They try to hurt him with the ball. Slowly, the other Dodgers begin to defend him. They begin to think of him as a member of the team, as a friend. Because of Jackie, the Brooklyn Dodgers win the last game of the season. That means they are going to play in the World Series. There is a big celebration in honor of Jackie Robinson. Brooklyn loves him. But to African-Americans, he is more than a great ball player. He is a great hero. He is proof that blacks can do anything whites can do.

It is not easy to be the first. Thanks to Jackie Robinson, there are now black players on every important baseball team. His courage opens the way for those who follow him.

Exercises

I. Vocabulary

You probably know many of these words from reading the story and looking at the pictures. If there are still some you don't know, look them up in your dictionary now.

hero	defend	innocent	rights
supposed (to)	team	equal	refuse
professional	bitter	insult	trial
liberty	arrest	courage	

II. Definitions

Try to guess the best definition for these words. Then look them up in your dictionary and draw a circle around the answer.

1. hero
   a. someone people pity
   b. someone people arrest
   c. someone people admire

2. to defend
   a. to agree
   b. to protect
   c. to punish

3. insult
   a. respect
   b. honor
   c. dishonor

4. professional
   a. doing something to earn a living
   b. doing something for fun
   c. doing something part time

5. (on) trial
   a. examination of facts in a law court
   b. punishment by law
   c. is guilty under the law

6. courage
   a. with anger
   b. with fear
   c. without fear

III. Reading Comprehension

Read the questions. Find the answers in the story. Write the answers under the questions.

1. What great honor does Jackie get at the University of California?

   _____

   _____

2. How does Jackie feel when the bus driver orders him to move to the back of the bus?

   _____

   _____

3. What does Jackie know he is not good at?

   _____

   _____

4. What is Branch Rickey's plan?

   _____

   _____

5. After he wins many games, how do the other Dodgers begin to think of Jackie?

   _____

   _____

6. How do African-Americans feel about him?

   _____

   _____

IV. Discussion
Look at the pictures. Talk to your partner. Use words from the story.

Picture #1.
Why is Jackie Robinson different from most blacks in the army?

Picture #2.
What does Jackie do to have this great celebration in Brooklyn?

V. Writing

Dictation. Study the first paragraph of the story. As you write, be careful about punctuation. Close your book as the teacher dictates. Then open your book and check your work.

_____

_____

_____

_____

_____

"Dirkson? Dirkson? I don't know that name. Who is he?"

Waiting for Dr. Dirkson

A Play

THE SCENE: A classroom in a high school. Summer is over. This is the first day of school. The students arrive one by one or in small groups. Everyone stops to read the sign on the door. It says: PHYSICS 1, DR. F. DIRKSON.

THE CHARACTERS: Various students (Linda, Ben, Rudy, Tony, Molly) and Dr. Dirkson.

Linda: Dirkson? Dirkson? I don't know that name. Who is he?

Rudy: Don't ask me. He must be a new teacher. I don't remember him teaching in this school last year. Do you, Ben?

Ben: No, but here comes Tony. He knows everything. If anyone can tell you about Dr. What's-His-Name, Tony can.

Tony: (laughs.) I don't know everything. I only know almost everything. What is your question, please?

Molly: What do you know about this new teacher?

Tony: I don't really know much about Dr. Dirkson. I do hear things, though. I hear lots of things.

Rudy: What do you hear? Is he a good teacher? I'm hoping to go to college. This class is important to me.

Tony: I have a friend who goes to Central High School. I'm almost sure that's where Dr. Dirkson comes from. If it's the same teacher, he is rough. Believe me, he is rough and tough.

Linda: What do you mean 'rough and tough'? I plan to go to college, too. I have to do well in this class.

Tony: What I hear is that Dirkson's tests are very hard. He usually fails about half the class. All the girls.

Linda: (angry) That can't be true. You're making it up, Tony.

Molly:	He's just talking like that to annoy us, Linda. Tony, What does Dr. Dirkson look like? Is he married?
Tony:	I don't think so. But don't get excited, Molly. He isn't going to interest you. He's about seventy-seven years old and he uses a walking stick.
Molly:	(she is angry) Tony, why do you say that this teacher fails all the girls? Do you think physics is too hard for girls? Do you think we can't do it?
Tony:	All I'm saying, Molly, is that girls don't make it in Dr. Dirkson's class. Physics is very difficult. It's not like art or music or history. It's a science. How many famous women scientists are there? Hardly any. You can count them on the fingers of one hand.
Ben:	That's not fair, Tony. There are many women who are doctors and engineers and scientists. And there are more of them all the time.
Rudy:	That's right, Tony. I agree with Ben. Girls can do anything we can do.
Tony:	I don't care what anybody says. I'm telling you the truth, Molly. I'm not saying that girls are not intelligent. They just don't have the right kind of intelligence to understand physics. Dr. Dirkson must know that. Take my advice and get out of his class before he walks in.
	(A very pretty young woman hurries into the classroom.)
Dr. Dirkson:	Good morning. I'm sorry I'm late. I am Dr. Dirkson.
	(The whole class starts to laugh. Everyone laughs hard. Everyone except Tony.)

Exercises

I. Vocabulary

You probably know many of these words from reading the story and looking at the pictures. If there are still some you don't know, look them up in your dictionary now.

scene	annoy	sign	various
physics	important	rough	group
count	fail		

II. Definitions

Try to guess the best definition for these words. Then look them up in your dictionary and draw a circle around the answer.

1. various
   a. a couple
   b. a crowd
   c. several

2. rough
   a. easy
   b. difficult
   c. smart

3. fail
   a. advance
   b. fall
   c. flunk

4. to annoy
   a. to please
   b. to cheer
   c. trouble

5. physics
   a. science
   b. art
   c. music

6. to count
   a. to number
   b. to tell
   c. to repeat

III. Reading Comprehension

Read the questions. Find the answers in the story. Write the answers under the questions.

1. What do the students read on the classroom door?

   _____

   _____

2. What does Tony say he knows about Dr. Dirkson?

   _____

   _____

3. What does Tony say he hears about Dr. Dirkson's tests?

   _____

   _____

4. What does Molly ask Tony about why this teacher fails all the girls?

   _____

   _____

5. What does Tony say about the kind of intelligence girls have?

   _____

   _____

6. Why does everyone in the class laugh, except Tony, when the door opens?

   _____

   _____

IV. Discussion

Look at the pictures. Talk to your partner. Use words from the story.

Picture #1.
What is Tony telling his friends?
Why do they look so unhappy?

Picture #2.
At this moment, what are the students thinking?
Who is Dr. F. Dirkson?
Why do you think Tony isn't laughing like everyone else?

V. Writing

Write four things that Tony thinks he knows about Dr. Dirkson.

1. _____

2. _____

3. _____

4. _____

"This is the melon of my dreams."

The Melon of His Dreams

Mr. Maggio is eighty-six years old. He does not work any more, but he is very busy just the same. Every day he walks to two or three markets. Sometimes four. He is always searching for the most beautiful fruit, the most perfect vegetables. Finding them isn't easy. It takes a lot of time.

Most of the people who work in markets know him. Winter or summer, Mr. Maggio wears the same black suit and gray hat. When he comes into the vegetable department, the men and women who work there look at each other. They hope he is not going to cause any trouble today.

One day, at one of the markets, a customer is choosing tomatoes and putting them in a bag. To her surprise, Mr. Maggio takes a tomato away from her. He smells it and makes a disgusted face.

"Do you call this a tomato?" he asks in a loud voice. All the customers in the vegetable department turn around to look at him. "This is not a tomato. It looks like a tomato but it tastes like a wet towel. I remember the tomatoes in Italy. So red! So juicy! Such a wonderful smell! Italian tomatoes are real tomatoes!"

The same day, but in another market, Mr. Maggio is not able to find perfect oranges. He thinks he sees better ones at the bottom of the pile. When he digs down to get them, the whole pile of oranges spills. Soon there are oranges rolling on the floor all over the market.

Mr. Franchetti, the market manager, comes over to speak to the old man. "Mr. Maggio," he says patiently, "can you please tell me what is wrong with the oranges on top of the pile?"

"Do you call these oranges?" Mr. Maggio cries. "Look how green they are! Look how small they are! No, my friend. I remember the oranges in Italy. Yellow as the sun! Sweet as sugar! Those oranges are real oranges!"

Mr. Franchetti is getting angry. "I come from Italy too," he says. "I don't remember that Italian oranges are any better than the ones we sell right here in this market."

By this time, everyone in the market is listening. Mr. Maggio tells the manager, "If you don't know the difference between good oranges and bad oranges, I pity you. I feel sorry for you."

"Do me a favor," says Mr. Franchetti to Mr. Maggio. "Next time buy your oranges somewhere else. Don't come back to this market."

But after a few days, Mr. Maggio forgets and comes back. He is looking for strawberries that are fat and dark red, and for bananas without any brown spots.

Now it is summer. All the markets have many different kinds of melons. Big ones. Little ones. Round ones. Long ones. Of all the fruits, Mr. Maggio loves melons best. He gets tired from walking to so many markets in such hot weather. He smells all the melons. He shakes them. He pinches them. He spoils the neat piles in which they are arranged. Never does he find a melon good enough to buy.

"I remember the melons in Italy," Mr. Maggio says sadly. "When you eat such a melon, you think you are already in heaven. A melon like that is the melon of my dreams."

"I have a good idea," says Mr. Franchetti one day. "In August I am going to Italy to visit my mother. I can bring you back a melon, if you want."

Mr. Maggio can hardly believe that someone wants to do such a wonderful thing for him.

Mr. Franchetti has three weeks vacation. Every day, Mr. Maggio goes to the market to see if the manager is back yet. No, not yet. Finally, though, he does come back and he has a round package for Mr. Maggio.

The old man's hands shake as he tears open the paper and takes out the melon. He can't wait to taste it. He asks Mr. Franchetti for a knife and cuts a small piece. As he bites it, his eyes close with pleasure.

"This is the melon of my dreams!" he cries. "At last I am a happy man. Dear Mr. Franchetti, my best friend in the world, how can I thank you?"

"Don't thank me. Just go home and enjoy it," says Mr. Franchetti kindly.

When the old man is gone, Mr. Franchetti speaks to one of his workers.

"Do you know where that melon comes from, Jim?"

"Sure I know," says Jim. "From Italy."

"Jim," says Mr. Franchetti, "do I look like a fool? Do you really think I am going to carry a melon all the way from Italy to the United States?"

"Where does it come from, then?" asks Jim.

Mr. Franchetti points to the pile of melons behind him.

"Right from this market, from the top of that pile," he says. And he smiles a big smile.

Exercises

I. Vocabulary

You probably know many of these words from reading the story and looking at the pictures. If there are still some you don't know, look them up in your dictionary now.

cause	search(ing)	manager	busy
disgusted	patient(ly)	department	juicy
pity	choose	pile	sorry

II. Definitions

Try to guess the best definition for these words. Then look them up in your dictionary and draw a circle around the answer.

1. busy
   - a. feeling happy
   - b. doing something
   - c. going somewhere

2. to cause
   - a. to make (something) happen
   - b. to follow something
   - c. to have something

3. patiently
   - a. anxiously
   - b. not anxiously
   - c. cheerfully

4. pile(of)
   - a. a large amount of
   - b. a hill of
   - c. a lot of

5. to search
   - a. to find
   - b. to need
   - c. to look for

6. sorry
   - a. mad
   - b. glad
   - c. sad

III. Reading Comprehension

Read the questions. Find the answers in the story. Write the answers under the questions.

1. Where does Mr. Maggio go every day?

   _____

   _____

2. Why do the men and women who work in the vegetable department look at each other when Mr. Maggio comes in?

   _____

   _____

3. What does Mr. Maggio remember about oranges in Italy?

   _____

   _____

4. What good idea does Mr. Franchetti tell to Mr. Maggio?

   _____

   _____

5. What does Mr. Maggio say when he tastes a piece of the melon?

   _____

   _____

6. From where does the melon come? What does Mr. Franchetti tell Jim?

   _____

   _____

IV. Discussion

Look at the pictures. Talk to your partner. Use words from the story.

Picture #1.
What is Mr. Maggio doing?
What does he say to the surprised customer?

Picture #2.
What is Mr. Maggio doing?
What does he say to Mr. Franchetti?

V. Writing

Dictation. Study the first paragraph in the story for a few minutes. Think about spelling and punctuation. Then write below as the teacher dictates. When you finish, turn back to the paragraph and check your work. Correct your mistakes.

_____

_____

_____

_____

_____

Joseph travels to Washington, D.C. to speak for himself and his tribe.

I Will Fight No More Forever
The Story of Chief Joseph of the Nez Perce Indians

For ten thousand years, and maybe more, the beautiful green Wallowa Valley is home to a tribe, or group, of Nez Perce Indians. The Wallowa Valley is in part of the United States we now call Oregon. The Nez Perces live and hunt and fish here, and for many, many miles all around.

By 1850, white people are coming west. They want land for themselves. The United States government does in Oregon what it is doing all over the country. It makes plans to take Native Americans, or Indians, off their land to 'reservations' where they must remain. Reservations are land that the government reserves, or puts aside, for Indians. On these reservations, Indians are supposed to learn to farm like the white man. They are supposed to go to school and to church, and to forget the ways of their people. The government promises money and gifts to Indian tribes if they agree to go to reservations. Over the years, Nez Perce chiefs meet many times to discuss this with men of the United States government.

In 1871, Joseph becomes chief of the Wallowa Nez Perces. His Indian name is Hin-mah-too-yah-lat-kekt, which means Thunder Rolling In The Mountains. He is a big man, over six feet tall and very strong. Joseph is handsome, intelligent, kind and just. He is a man of peace who becomes a man of war when he has to. Chief Joseph and his people do not want to accept money or gifts. They do not want to go to a reservation. Joseph remembers his father's last advice to him:

"My son, never forget my dying words. This country holds your father's body. Never sell the bones of your father and mother."

In 1877, General Howard of the United States Army calls the Nez Perces to still another meeting. Joseph arrives wearing his best clothes. There are stripes of red paint on his face. Even his horse is striped red. He looks like the great leader he is, but in his heart he is sad and afraid. He doesn't want to sell the home of his father's fathers. But he also wants to avoid war with the powerful Americans. He tries to make General Howard understand.

"I do not believe," he says, "that the Great Spirit (God) gives one kind of men the right to tell another kind of men what they must do."

General Howard feels sympathy for Chief Joseph. Howard writes to the government in Washington, D.C., the capital of the United States: "I think it is a great mistake to take from Joseph and his band (tribe) of Nez Perce Indians that valley... Let these really peaceable Indians have this poor valley for their own." But General Howard takes his orders from the United States government. Those orders are that the Nez Perces have thirty days to move to a reservation. If they do not go peacefully, they must be forced to go.

Joseph believes his people are too weak to fight the United States. He is ready to obey Howard, but many of his people are not. Three Nez Perces kill three white men. Whites who live close by want the army to punish the Indians. Chief Joseph knows soldiers are coming soon. To protect his people, he quickly takes them away. So begins the famous journey of the Nez Perce Indians. Chief Joseph leads seven hundred men, women and children seventeen hundred miles toward freedom in Canada. With General Howard's soldiers chasing them, they cross high mountains and wild rivers. They fight five big battles with the United States Army and win four of them. Joseph is a leader with so much courage that even his enemies respect and admire him.

The Nez Perces can win battles, but Joseph knows they cannot win this war. He pushes his people to travel faster toward Canada. They must get far ahead of the army. The time comes when General Howard is two days behind the Indians. Joseph feels safe and allows his people to rest for the night in the Bear's Paw Mountains. After twenty weeks, the Nez Perces are too tired to walk any more. Anyway, it is only forty-five miles to Canada. What can happen now?

The Indians do not completely understand the power of the telegraph lines, which they call 'singing wires'. General Howard sends a telegraph message to Army Colonel Miles, who is closer to Bear's Paw Mountains. Howard tells him to stop the Nez Perces before they reach Canada. With six hundred soldiers, fresh horses and very big guns called cannons, Miles finds Chief Joseph. The

Nez Perces fight bravely for five days, but it is hopeless. Joseph gives himself up to Miles. He asks only to go home to his own country after the war.

"I am tired of fighting," he says. "The little children are freezing to death. My people have no blankets, no food. Hear me, my chiefs. My heart is sick and sad. From where the sun now stands, I will fight no more forever." So ends the last and the greatest of the Indian wars.

Colonel Miles promises to let the Nez Perces return to their own country. He writes to the head of the army. But the government does not allow Chief Joseph to go home. He is sent to a reservation in Kansas, far, far away from Oregon. Joseph travels to Washington, D.C. to speak for himself and his tribe.

"I know that my race (people) must change," he says. "We cannot hold our own with white men as we are. We only ask an even chance to live as other men live. Let me be a free man—free to travel, free to work, free to follow the religion of my fathers, free to think and act and talk for myself. Then we shall all be alike— brothers of one father and one mother, with one sky above us and one government for all."

Those great words move the hearts of many people, even some in government. They send Chief Joseph to a reservation in the state of Washington, nearer to Oregon. But he never returns to his beloved valley. He is never again a really free man.

Exercises

I. Vocabulary
You probably know many of these words from reading the story and looking at the pictures. If there are still some you don't know, look them up in your dictionary now.

free(ly)	avoid	battle	government
sympathy	war	just	capital
allow	advice	orders	punish
power			

II. Definitions
Try to guess the best definition for these words. Then look them up in your dictionary and draw a circle around the answer.

1. to be just
   - a. to be false
   - b. to be fair
   - c. to be funny

2. to avoid
   - a. to overdo
   - b. to deceive
   - c. to keep away from

3. sympathy
   - a. pity
   - b. kindness
   - c. helpfulness

4. allow
   - a. permit
   - b. pay
   - c. pray for

5. punish
   - a. sue
   - b. apologize
   - c. make (someone) suffer

6. powerful
   - a. strong
   - b. governing
   - c. supporting

III. Reading Comprehension

Read the questions. Find the answers in the story. Write the answers under the questions.

1. What do the Nez Perce Indians do in the beautiful green Wallowa Valley?

   _____

   _____

2. What are Indians supposed to do on reservations?

   _____

   _____

3. Why do Chief Joseph and his people not accept money or gifts from the U.S. government?

   _____

   _____

4. Why do the Nez Perces stop in Bear's Paw Mountains?

   _____

   _____

5. What does Joseph say to the government about his people?

   _____

   _____

6. Where does Joseph live the last part of his life?

   _____

   _____

IV. Discussion
Look at the pictures. Talk to your partner.
Use words from the story.

Picture #1.
Where are the Indians trying to go?
Why are they stopping here?
How far do they still need to travel?

Picture #2.
How is General Howard able to ask
Colonel Miles to stop the Nez Perces?
Do the Indians fight long?
Why do they give up?

V. Writing
Dictation. Study the first paragraph. As you write, be careful about punctuation.
Close your book as the teacher dictates. Then open your book and check your work.

_____

_____

_____

_____

_____

Word List

This comprehensive word list includes vocabulary from the stories which might be new to some advanced primary level students. Cognates of Spanish are here marked "C." Words found in the *Oxford Picture Dictionary of American English* are marked "O." Those found in Robert J. Dixson's *The 2,000 Most Frequently Used Words In English* are marked "D."

A

accident	C		D
act	C	O	D
admire	C		D
admit			D
advertisement			D
advice			D
afraid			D
agree			D
allow			D
angel	C		D
angry			D
animal	C	O	D
annoy			D
anxious	C		D
anyhow			D
apartment	C	O	
apple		O	
appointment			D
arrange			D
arrest	C		D
arrive			D
aspirin	C		
audience	C	O	D
avoid			D

B

bag		O	D
bake		O	
bank	C	O	D
barber		O	
barn		O	
baseball		O	
basket			D
basketball		O	
battle	C		D

beach		O	D
bed		O	D
beg			D
behind		O	D
belong			D
bench		O	
bend			D
bite			D
bitter			D
blade		O	
blanket		O	
blind			D
blood			D
bone			D
bore			D
bottom			D
branch		O	D
breakfast			D
breath			D
brown			D
burn		O	D
busy			D
butter		O	D
butterfly		O	

C

camel	C	O	
camera	C	O	D
capital	C		D
carry		O	D
cause	C		D
celebrate	C		D
chain		O	D
chance			D
change			D
cheerful			D

chicken		O	D
chimney	C	O	
choose			D
church			D
clean		O	D
climb			D
coal		O	D
complain			D
confuse			D
control			D
cook		O	D
corn		O	D
corner		O	
cough			D
count	C		D
courage	C		D
cow		O	D
crowd			D
crutch		O	
cry			D
curious	C		D
custom	C		D
cut		O	D

D

death			D
decide	C		D
deep			D
defend	C	O	D
deliver		O	D
department		O	D
desert	C	O	D
dig		O	D
direct(ly)			D
disappear	C		D
disappointed			D

103

	C	O	D
disgusted			D
distance	C		D
disturb	C		D
dozen			D
dream			D
dress			D
drugstore		O	
E			
earth		O	D
easy			D
edge			D
egg		O	
elephant	C	O	
end			D
engineer	C	O	D
entertainment	C		D
equal	C		D
escape	C		D
excited			D
expect			D
F			
factory		O	D
fail			D
faint			D
famous	C		D
fan			D
farm		O	D
favor	C		D
fear			D
fence		O	D
field		O	
fill			D
find			D
fire		O	D
fireplace		O	
flashlight		O	
floor		O	D
fly		O	D
fool			D
forever			D
forget			D
form			D
fortune	C		D
free			D
friendly			D
frighten			D

	C	O	D
G			
game			D
garage	C	O	D
garden		O	D
gate			D
glasses		O	
government	C		D
granddaughter		O	D
grandson		O	D
grapefruit		O	
grass		O	D
grave			D
green		O	D
group	C		D
grow			D
guard	C		D
guess			D
H			
hand		O	D
handsome			D
hang		O	D
happy			D
hardly			D
hate			D
hay		O	D
head		O	D
heart		O	D
heaven			D
hero	C		D
hide			D
hill		O	D
homeplate		O	
honor	C		D
hospital	C	O	D
hungry			D
hunt			D
hurry			D
husband		O	D
I			
ice			D
ice cream cone		O	
idea	C		D
imagine	C		D
important	C		D
innocent	C		
insist	C		D

	C	O	D
insult	C		D
intelligent	C		
invite	C		D
iron			D
J			
jar		O	
jelly		O	
job			D
joke			D
juice			D
just	C		
K			
key			D
kind			D
kitchen		O	D
knee		O	D
knife		O	D
knock			D
L			
laboratory	C		
land			D
lead			D
lean			D
leg		O	D
lie			D
light			D
lion	C	O	D
living room		O	
lock		O	
lone		O	D
lost			D
lucky			D
M			
manager		O	D
market		O	D
mask	C	O	
mechanic	C	O	D
melon	C	O	D
milk			D
mistake			D
monkey		O	
mother		O	D
move(r)		O	D

N

	C	O	D
neat			D
neck		O	D
nest			D
net		O	
notice			D

O

	C	O	D
officer	C	O	D
oil		O	D
orange		O	D
order	C		D
own			D

P

	C	O	D
package		O	D
pail		O	
pan		O	D
paper	C	O	D
patient(ly)	C		D
paw		O	
peaceful			D
peel		O	
physics	C		
pick		O	D
piece		O	D
pile			D
pinch			D
pipe	C	O	
pity			D
plant	C	O	D
pleasure	C		D
popular	C		D
potato	C	O	
power	C		D
powerful			D
present			D
prison	C		D
professional	C		
promise	C		D
proof			D
proud			D
pull			D
punish			D

Q

	C	O	D
quarrel			D
question			D
quick			D

R

	C	O	D
rain		O	D
reach			D
recognize	C		D
refuse			D
religious	C		D
remember			D
remind			D
repeat	C		D
rescue			D
respect	C		D
reward			D
rights			D
ring		O	D
roll			D
roof		O	D
rope		O	
rough			D
rub			D
rule			D

S

	C	O	D
sad(ly)			D
sand		O	D
save			D
scene	C		D
science	C	O	D
search			D
send			D
separation	C		D
shake			D
share			D
shine			D
shirt		O	D
shoot		O	D
shoulder		O	
sign			D
skin		O	D
slave			D
smell			D
smile			D
smoke		O	D
snake		O	
soil			D
sorry			D
soup	C		D
speak			D
spill			D
spoil			D
spot			D
stage		O	D
star		O	D
stove	C	O	D
strange	C		D
strawberry		O	
string			D
sun		O	D
supposed			D
surprise	C		D
swallow			D
sweet			D
sword		O	D
sympathy	C		D

T

	C	O	D
team		O	D
tear			D
telegraph	C		
thin			D
think			D
threaten			D
throat		O	
ticket		O	D
toe		O	D
tomato	C	O	D
toothbrush		O	
touch		O	D
towel	C	O	D
trial			D
trick			D
trouble			D
truckdriver		O	

U

	C	O	D
ugly			D
uniform	C	O	

V

	C	O	D
vacation	C		D
various	C		D
vegetable	C	O	D
village			D
visit	C		D
voice	C		D

Word	O	D		Word	O	D		Word	O	D
W				wheat	O	D		worry		D
wait		D		whip		D		wrong		D
wall	O	D		whisper		D		**Y**		
war		D		whole		D		yard		D D
weak		D		widow		D		year		D D
weather	O	D		wise		D		yellow		D
weight	O	D		wonder		D				
wet		D		world	O	D				

Exercise Answer Key

THE LITTLE TEACHER

Exercise II
1. b   4. a
2. c   5. c
3. a   6. b

Exercise III
1. He sends her an airplane ticket to come to America.
2. He is the child with brown skin and black hair who lives in the apartment below.
3. Everyday after school, Javier teaches Lin-mei the new English words he is learning.
4. Lin-mei gladly agrees to take care of Javier.
5. Suddenly Lin-mei discovers that there are many interesting things to do in Boston.
6. "Why don't I cook a Chinese dinner?" Lin-mei thinks.

LUCKY & UNLUCKY

Exercise II
1. a   4. b
2. c   5. a
3. a   6. b

Exercise III
1. They call him that because he always finds things.
2. He hides it in a safe place.
3. "You're going to have very good luck."
4. Because black cats are supposed to bring bad luck.
5. Her husband is dead and she has no children. Her life is lonely without her cat.
6. Because she can see that Lucky likes the cat. She hates to take her away from Lucky.

A DOUBLE CHOCOLATE ICE CREAM CONE

Exercise II
1. b   4. a
2. c   5. c
3. c   6. a,b,c

Exercise III
1. She always reads during the Friday lunches.
2. Gregory Gordon is famous for his bright blue eyes, coal black hair and beautiful, deep voice.
3. In August, the movie company arrives with big trucks and many lights and cameras and dozens of busy people.
4. Her hands are shaking, her face is hot, her feet are cold, and her heart is beating one hundred and thirty times a minute.
5. She tries not to look at Gregory Gordon.
6. "Your ice cream cone is in your purse," he says.

BABY FLIES AWAY

Exercise II
1. a   4. a,b,c
2. c   5. c
3. a   6. c

Exercise III
1. Baby travels to the new house in the car with the family.
2. Up a tree she goes.
3. Mr. Sullivan throws the rope over the tree. He hopes to pull the top of the tree down low. When it is low enough, he plans to reach Baby and rescue her.
4. Baby goes flying through the air.
5. The first thing Andy notices at the Rose house is their big, beautiful cat.
6. Because she comes directly from heaven.

MOTHER AND DAUGHTER

Exercise II

1. c   4. b
2. a   5. a
3. c   6. a,b,c

Exercise III

1. She is calling somebody on the telephone.
2. Because she has a terrible cold.
3. She can go to the market.
4. For a mother, nothing is too much.
5. No, she has a granddaughter.
6. She should put on her glasses.

A WOMAN'S WORK

Exercise II

1. b   4. a
2. a   5. a
3. c   6. c

Exercise III

1. Green grass and little flowers grow on it.
2. "My work is hard," Laszlo reminds Maruska, "and your work is easy."
3. He finds the pail of milk lying on its side. All the milk is gone. Katya is wet with milk from her head to her toes.
4. She can eat the good green grass that grows there.
5. He is afraid she may fall off and break her leg.
6. Her weight on the rope pulls Laszlo half way up the chimney.
7. Laszlo falls down the chimney right into the big pot of water.

THE APPOINTMENT

Exercise II

1. b   4. c
2. a   5. a
3. a,b,c 6. a

Exercise III

1. Many people believe on this day the dead come back to earth to visit their families.
2. "Take off your mask, friend, and let me see who you are."
3. "Puebla is a big city. I can hide there. I can surely escape Death there."
4. It is not time yet.
5. He has an appointment with someone else.
6. Because he has an appointment with Emilio late tonight in Puebla.

THE BLIND MEN AND THE ELEPHANT

Exercise II

1. c   4. b
2. b   5. a
3. a   6. c

Exercise III

1. Life is good to them. They like each other and help each other.
2. They are especially excited about the elephant.
3. One at a time, they touch Ravi to discover what he looks like.
4. They are too busy quarreling to listen.
5. Because every one of the six blind men is sure that only he is right, and that the others are wrong.
6. They are probably quarreling at this very minute.

MARYJO GETS A RIDE HOME

Exercise II

1. b   4. a
2. a,b,c, 5. a
3. c   6. b

Exercise III

1. Tonight it is raining so hard that he often can't see the road.
2. "I try and try to call them but they never answer."
3. She is not in the truck. She is not near the truck. She is not anywhere.

4. "It happens every year on this date. My poor girl tries so hard to come home on her birthday, but she never, never comes."
5. She leads the way among the graves of the dead and stops in front of a white gravestone.
6. There is something hanging on the corner of Maryjo's gravestone. It is his jacket.

ANDROCLES AND THE LION
Exercise II
1. c   4. a
2. a,b,c,   5. c
3. b   6. a
Exercise III
1. Antonius makes Androcles work hard night and day.
2. Androcles runs away as fast as he can.
3. He pulls the splinter out.
4. The lion hunts and shares the meat with Androcles.
5. Because the audience enjoys seeing the hungry lions eat criminals.
6. He stops, remembers him and begins to lick his face.

JACKIE ROBINSON PLAYS BALL
Exercise II
1. b,c   4. a
2. b   5. a
3. c   6. c
Exercise III
1. He becomes an "All American."
2. He is insulted.
3. He knows he is not good at accepting insults.
4. To bring Jackie Robinson to play with the Brooklyn Dodgers.
5. They begin to think of him as a member of the team, as a friend.
6. He is more than a great ball player. He is a great hero. He is proof that blacks can do anything whites can do.

WAITING FOR DR. DIRKSON
Exercise II
1. c   4. c
2. b   5. a
3. c   6. a
Exercise III
1. Physics 1, Dr. F. Dirkson.
2. "I don't really know much about Dr. Dirkson."
3. "Dr. Dirkson's tests are very hard. He usually fails about half the class. All the girls."
4. "Do you think physics is too hard for girls? Do you think we can't do it?"
5. "I'm not saying that girls are not intelligent. They just don't have the right kind of intelligence to understand physics."
6. Because Dr. Dirkson is a young woman.

MELON OF HIS DREAMS
Exercise II
1. b   4. a,b,c
2. a   5. c
3. b   6. c
Exercise III
1. Every day he walks to two or three markets.
2. They hope he is not going to cause any trouble today.
3. "Oranges in Italy are yellow as the sun! Sweet as sugar! Those oranges are real oranges!"
4. "In August I am going to Italy to visit my mother. I can bring you a melon if you want."
5. "This is the melon of my dreams," he cries.
6. "Right from this market, from the top of that pile."

I WILL FIGHT NO MORE FOREVER

Exercise II

1. b   4. a
2. c   5. c
3. a   6. a

Exercise III

1. The Nez Perces live and hunt and fish here, and for many, many miles all around.
2. Indians are supposed to learn to farm like the white man. They are supposed to go to school and to church, and to forget the ways of their people.
3. They do not want to go to a reservation.
4. After twenty weeks, the Nez Perces are too tired to walk any more.
5. "I know that my race (people) must change," he says. "We cannot hold our own with white men as we are."
6. He must live the rest of his life on an Indian reservation in the state of Washington, never again a really free man.

ABOUT THE AUTHOR

For many years, Judith Bailey was a teacher, and most particularly, a reading teacher, in the Los Angeles Unified School District. Under an ESAA grant, she worked with hundreds of newly arrived students who spoke little or no English. Books, reading, the whole spectrum of language arts, have been her life-long preoccupation. Before becoming a teacher, she was a story analyst and associate story editor in several motion picture studios.

She now lives in Forestville, California, where she occupies herself as a free lance writer for major educational publishers.

ABOUT THE ARTIST

Meredith Kraike is a free lance illustrator and fine artist. She has a Bachelor of Fine Arts degree in printing and printmaking from Memphis College of Arts and a Master of Fine Arts degree from the University of Oregon.

For almost ten years she taught printing and drawing to adults and children in Seattle, Washington, where she continues to work as an illustrator today.